THE D-DAY INVASION OF NORMANDY

THE D-DAY INVASION OF NORMANDY

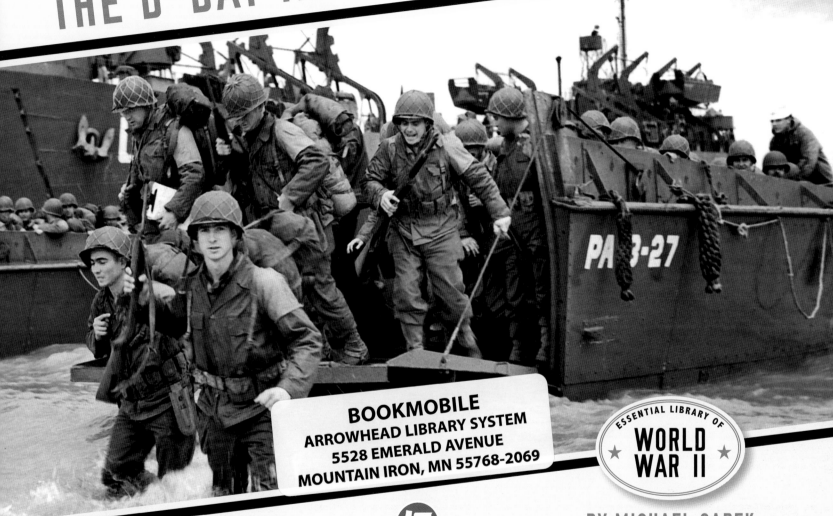

PA 3-27

ESSENTIAL LIBRARY OF
WORLD WAR II

Essential Library

An Imprint of Abdo Publishing
abdopublishing.com

BY MICHAEL CAPEK

CONTENT CONSULTANT

PETER MANSOOR
ASSOCIATE PROFESSOR
GENERAL RAYMOND E. MASON JR.
CHAIR IN MILITARY HISTORY
THE OHIO STATE UNIVERSITY

abdopublishing.com

Published by Abdo Publishing, a division of ABDO, PO Box 398166, Minneapolis, Minnesota 55439. Copyright © 2016 by Abdo Consulting Group, Inc. International copyrights reserved in all countries. No part of this book may be reproduced in any form without written permission from the publisher. Essential Library™ is a trademark and logo of Abdo Publishing.

Printed in the United States of America, North Mankato, Minnesota

052015
092015

Cover Photo: Time Life Pictures/US Coast Guard/The LIFE Picture Collection/Getty Images
Interior Photos: Time Life Pictures/US Coast Guard/The LIFE Picture Collection/Getty Images, 1, 3; US Air Force, 6, 9, 12; Sgt. Johnson/IWM/Getty Images, 11, 99 (top); AP Images, 14, 27, 41, 44, 54, 82, 85, 88, 93, 98 (bottom), 99 (bottom); Library of Congress, 19, 23, 32, 47; Berliner Verlag/Archiv/Picture-Alliance/DPA/AP Images, 21, 17, 79, 98 (top); SeM/UIG/Getty Images, 25; Bettmann/Corbis, 29, 97; US Army, 34, 36, 74, 72–73; US National Archives and Records Administration, 39, 64, 66, 87, 91; US Army Signal Corps/AP Images, 50; MPI/Getty Images, 55; US Navy, 56, 62, 65 (right), 70, 77; PhotoQuest/Getty Images, 61; Frederic Lewis/Getty Images, 65 (left); US Military, 81

Editor: Arnold Ringstad
Series Designers: Kelsey Oseid and Maggie Villaume

Library of Congress Control Number: 2015930967

Cataloging-in-Publication Data

Capek, Michael.
 The D-Day invasion of Normandy / Michael Capek.
  p. cm. -- (Essential library of World War II)
Includes bibliographical references and index.
ISBN 978-1-62403-792-4
1. Normandy (France)--Juvenile literature. 2. World War, 1939-1945--France--Normandy--Juvenile literature.   I. Title.
940.54--dc23

2015930967

CONTENTS

Towed gliders enable troops to make swift and silent landings behind enemy lines.

CHAPTER ★ 1 ★

THUNDER OVER NORMANDY

For soldiers in World War II, glider landings were always dangerous. In these engineless aircraft, used to silently carry troops behind enemy lines, every landing was a crash landing. But gliders would be critical components of the Allied invasion of Normandy, France, in the summer of 1944. For four years, Nazi Germany had dominated the European continent. Now, Allied troops from the United States, the United Kingdom, and Canada prepared to liberate France. Hundreds of thousands of troops would arrive on Normandy's beaches in landing craft on the morning of June 6, 1944, the day known as D-Day. But hours earlier, a few thousand soldiers would parachute or glide behind Nazi lines to accomplish important missions ahead of the main invasion force.

GLIDERS

Horsa gliders had a wingspan of 88 feet (27 m) and hinged nose panels so jeeps or other wheeled vehicles could be loaded and unloaded easily.[1] The gliders were constructed from wood, making them lightweight and relatively inexpensive to build. It also meant they would not use steel, which was needed for other, more heavily armored vehicles.

An elite company of British soldiers understood the risks that came along with glider missions. They also recognized the immense size of the task ahead of the Allied armies. Still, they had volunteered for a special mission. They would be among the first Allied soldiers to set foot on French soil on D-Day.

The company flew in six British-built Horsa gliders, each carrying 30 men. They were towed across the English Channel toward the French coast by powerful Allied transport aircraft. Below them in the stormy channel, the men caught occasional glimpses of white streaks. They were the wakes left by the vast array of ships headed for Normandy.

DESCENDING INTO FRANCE

When the glider-towing aircraft reached the French coast, late on the night of June 5, they released their gliders. The tow aircraft turned back to the United Kingdom to pick up more men. The gliders soared on, heading toward their assigned landing zone near the Caen Canal and the Orne River. These bodies of water marked the eastern edge of the Allied invasion area. The glider forces were assigned the task of capturing two key bridges there: Bénouville and Ranville. The structures were only a few hundred yards apart. They had to be taken intact, since Allied troops would soon need them for their advance inland from the beaches.

Allied gliders came to a rest in the open fields of the Normandy countryside.

The gliders descended silently in a ragged, single-file line. Pilots slowed the planes as much as possible. Still, they were traveling approximately 90 miles per hour (145 kmh) as they prepared to touch down in moonlit fields. The men inside the aircraft interlocked arms and braced for the landing. The ground rushed up toward them.

One glider splintered to pieces as soon as it hit the dirt. The bottom was ripped away and the front canopy was smashed, knocking the pilots unconscious. The glider careened sideways as the men inside struggled to shield themselves from flying wood fragments, rocks, dirt, and sparks. The wreck finally came to rest nose-first against an entanglement of barbed wire at the far edge of the field.

PEGASUS BRIDGE

The Bénouville Bridge over the Caen Canal was later renamed "Pegasus Bridge," after the flying horse emblem worn by British airborne troops. Local authorities replaced the bridge in 1994, using the same design as the old bridge. The original structure was moved to a memorial museum nearby.

TAKING THE BRIDGES

Amazingly, few men were injured. They poured out through the side door and the gaping hole in the front of the plane and prepared to attack. Nearby, other gliders skidded to a halt. They were within a few yards of the German defenders guarding the bridges. Yet until British soldiers began firing and throwing grenades, the Germans had no idea enemy troops had arrived. A German guard who rushed outside after hearing a noise in the nearby fields became the first soldier to die in combat on D-Day.

Securing key bridges was one of the most important objectives in the early hours of the D-Day invasion.

Distinctive stripes enabled Allied aircraft to easily identify each other during the invasion.

Within 15 minutes, both bridges were secured. Only two of the men in the 180-man unit were killed, the first Allied soldiers to die during the invasion.[2] The seizure of the bridges, among the earliest Allied actions on D-Day, was quick, efficient, and almost mistake-free. Very little else would run as smoothly through the rest of that long day. By nightfall on June 6, thousands of German, British, Canadian, and American troops would lie dead on and around the beaches of Normandy.

STRIPES

With thousands of aircraft flying toward France on D-Day, Allied planners worried confusion could lead to aircraft being shot down by accident. To prevent this, the wings and fuselages of all Allied planes were painted with large black and white stripes just before D-Day. This would enable antiaircraft gunners on the ground and fellow pilots in the sky to quickly recognize friendly aircraft.

nearly the

DANGEROUS TIMES, DESPERATE MEASURES

In the spring of 1944, Europe was a closed fortress. German dictator Adolf Hitler described it this way, and he was essentially correct. In 1939, Germany's tanks, planes, and soldiers had swept into Poland, introducing the world to a new kind of warfare. The rapid, highly coordinated assault became known as blitzkrieg, German for "lightning war." Over the next several years, Germany used mobile armored warfare to stun and dominate the continent. While the world watched, Hitler's troops invaded 15 European nations by 1942.

Among the conquered countries was France, which surrendered in June 1940 and became German-occupied territory. For the French people, the occupation of their country by their German foes was a catastrophe. To see German troops parading triumphantly through the streets of Paris, their capital city, was nearly unbearable. Many French citizens formed secret groups that worked day and night to undermine the German occupation of their country. These loosely organized groups formed what became known as the French Resistance. The Resistance provided information and assistance to the Allies throughout the war and played a role in the invasion that would finally rid France and the world of Nazi oppression.

Having subdued France, Hitler next set his sights on the United Kingdom. He planned to pound the nation into submission with air attacks and then invade across the English Channel with ground troops on barges. In the summer and fall of 1940, the German Luftwaffe, or air force, launched an all-out aerial assault on southern England and London, the nation's capital. The ensuing fight between German and British aircraft was called the Battle of Britain. Thousands of British citizens died during relentless aerial bombing. However, the pilots of the Royal Air Force (RAF) prevailed. Unable to control the skies over the United Kingdom, Germany canceled its invasion plans. British prime minister Winston Churchill gave the pilots of the RAF full credit for saving the nation: "Never in the field of human conflict was so much owed by so many to so few."[1]

Discouraged that he was not able to break the spirit of the British people, Adolf Hitler turned to the east. In 1939, just before invading Poland, Germany had signed a nonaggression pact with the Soviet Union. The peace deal also included a secret agreement that the two nations would divide the conquered Polish territory between them. But in the summer of 1941, Hitler turned against the Soviet Union, launching an invasion of the vast nation. German troops

ADOLF HITLER

1889–1945

The person who made D-Day necessary was Adolf Hitler. His name still symbolizes destruction and hatred more than seven decades after his death. By 1934, Hitler and his Nazi Party henchmen had taken control of the German government. Hitler declared himself chancellor of Germany, but preferred the title Führer, meaning "leader."

Having taken control of every aspect of German life and culture, Hitler set his sights on the rest of Europe. He unleashed his military on Poland in 1939. His objective was not just to rule Europe but also to rid the world of Jewish people and others he believed inferior to what he considered the "master race." As Hitler's armies trampled across Europe, the rest of the world watched in horror as they slaughtered and enslaved millions.

As his military decisions and behavior became erratic, Hitler began losing followers, including some of his own generals. He survived numerous assassination attempts, but he refused to admit his own mistakes or give up any power or conquered territory.

In Hitler's mind, he and Germany were safe inside "Fortress Europe," a concept he had invented to describe his empire. Defended by his armies and the system of fortifications known as Atlantic Wall, he felt invincible. D-Day would prove how vulnerable the Atlantic Wall truly was.

17

pushed the Soviets back hundreds of miles, nearly reaching the capital city of Moscow.

THE UNITED STATES JOINS THE WAR

Many in the United States watched the events unfolding in Europe with dread. Most US citizens sympathized with and supported the United Kingdom and its allies. Still, US president Franklin D. Roosevelt continued to declare he would keep the United States out of the European war. But a new threat was brewing in the Pacific. In the 1930s, Japan began expanding its empire, invading China and threatening other nations in the region. Japan allied itself with Germany and Italy. In late 1941, Japan made a fateful decision to attempt to crush US opposition in the Pacific. Hoping to destroy the US Pacific fleet, it staged a surprise attack on the naval base at Pearl Harbor, Hawaii, in December 1941. The United States immediately declared war on Japan. Germany then declared war on the United States. The separate conflicts in Europe and the Pacific had become a single war. On one side were the Allies, including the United States, the United Kingdom, Canada, Australia, China, and the Soviet Union. Opposing them were the Axis powers, consisting of Germany, Italy, and Japan.

In 1940 and 1941, Allied commandos made small raids against German forces in France and other places. There was little benefit gained by these attacks, other than to prove to Hitler the Allies were capable of fighting back. A serious invasion was needed to gain a foothold in occupied Europe.

Roosevelt and Churchill had been talking about such an invasion for years. So had Soviet premier Joseph Stalin. He insisted opening up a second front in Europe was essential. This would force Germany to divide its forces, diverting some troops away from fighting the Soviet Red Army in the east to deal with other Allied troops in the west. Millions of Soviets had already died in the war. The Soviet people had suffered and sacrificed alone long enough, Stalin insisted.

To prove to Stalin they were taking action, the Allies decided to stage a major raid in August 1942 on the port city of Dieppe in northern France. A Canadian force of approximately 5,100 infantrymen and a tank regiment made up the bulk of the attack force, supported by 1,000 British commandos and 50 US Army Rangers.[2] The force crossed the English Channel aboard 237 British destroyers, troop ships, and equipment barges.[3] The ships also carried a number of small landing craft to bring troops ashore.

When Roosevelt signed the official declaration of war against Germany, he set the stage for the eventual invasion of Nazi-held Europe.

The craft spread out and prepared to land troops along an 11-mile (18 km) stretch of coastline.

A lack of proper communication and planning doomed the attack almost from the start. The Germans discovered the advancing force and opened fire, killing hundreds on the beaches. Of the 5,100 Canadian troops who came ashore, 3,367 were killed or taken prisoner. Another 275 British commandos became casualties.[4] The rest were forced to retreat to their ships. Dieppe was a major victory for the Germans and a total catastrophe for the Allies. Mounting another invasion attempt in 1942 or 1943 appeared impossible.

THE ATLANTIC WALL

Time was working against the Allies. Field Marshal Erwin Rommel of Germany was busy installing additional bunkers, artillery, and barriers along the European coastline. This string of fortifications became known as the Atlantic Wall. Additionally, German scientists and engineers were hard at work designing and testing new weapons they hoped would secure a Nazi victory. One was the powerful V-2 rocket. The bomb-tipped rocket would fly in a large arc, touching the edge of outer space before plummeting toward enemy cities at faster than the speed of sound. Among the most terrifying prospects was the Me 262, the world's first jet fighter aircraft. It could fly at more than 500 miles per hour (800 kmh), approximately 100 miles per hour (160 kmh) faster than any Allied fighter.[5] When it became ready for service in 1945, the jet would be difficult to shoot down. With it, Hitler's Luftwaffe might be able to secure dominance over the skies of Europe.

All of this meant an invasion had to come as soon as possible. It also had to be overwhelmingly successful, leading rapidly to a total Allied victory. Few believed Hitler would ever surrender. Hitler and his fanatical inner circle seemed as though they would fight to the death. Winning the war required the complete destruction of Hitler's war machine and the end of the German army's will and ability to defend its country.

In 1942, the return of Allied forces to the continent of Europe seemed beyond the realm of possibility. The Allies were simply not ready to attempt another invasion. Much had been learned from the Dieppe disaster, though. By the end of 1943, the situation was different. A smart, complex master plan had been developed. Men were better trained. Vast numbers of tanks, ships, and other equipment were being produced and assembled. The next attempt to invade Europe would make Dieppe look like a minor skirmish by comparison.

THE DEADLY CHANNEL

The English Channel is one of the most dangerous bodies of water in the world. Unpredictable weather, tides, and winds have made it a graveyard of ships for centuries. By the 1940s, no invasion fleet had dared cross the channel in nearly 300 years.[6] Even Hitler, who desperately wanted to invade England, decided a channel invasion was too risky, especially if the RAF still controlled the skies.

Infantry and tank crews trained intensively in the United States and the United Kingdom

HITLER'S ATLANTIC WALL

By 1944, Hitler's Atlantic Wall stretched for 3,000 miles (4,800 km) along the western edge of the European continent, from Norway in the north to France in the south. Rather than a single wall, it was actually composed of thousands of separate structures. Many of these were massive, steel-reinforced concrete bunkers protecting large and small artillery pieces facing the sea. Tunnels connected the bunkers and led to barracks and storage depots.

In addition, Rommel ordered various obstacles and barriers placed along beaches and the shoreline. Belgian gates, for example, were heavy steel fences. They were usually on rollers and could be moved into place to block tanks and other vehicles from coming ashore. Some beaches also bristled with hedgehogs, massive wooden or steel girders bolted or welded together and half buried in the sand at low tide. They jutted upwards and outwards to snag small boats or rip the bottoms out of landing craft. Tetrahydras, squat, pyramid-shaped obstacles made of concrete or steel, served the same purpose.

Explosives formed another line of defense in the Atlantic Wall. Rommel's soldiers attached Teller mines to many obstacles. These bombs exploded on contact. German troops placed more than 6.5 million mines on Normandy's beaches.[7] At high tide, most of these obstacles and mines were invisible, hidden just beneath the waterline.

General Dwight D. Eisenhower, *center*, assumed overall responsibility for the

CHAPTER 3

PLANNING THE INVASION

The Allied leadership appointed General Dwight D. Eisenhower of the United States chief of the Supreme Headquarters of the Allied Expeditionary Forces (SHAEF) in December 1943. By that time, the British had already assembled the details of a workable invasion plan. Although Eisenhower was supreme commander, much of the SHAEF staff was British. Sharing ideas and responsibilities between two major Allied nations created an atmosphere of teamwork and cooperation that was lacking among the Axis powers.

Eisenhower's deputy commander was British air chief marshal Arthur Tedder. British air vice marshal Trafford Leigh-Mallory was in charge of all air operations, and British admiral Bertram Ramsay commanded Operation Neptune, the vast naval phase of the invasion. The whole invasion was given the code name

Overlord. British General Bernard Montgomery directed all Allied ground forces. US General Omar Bradley was placed in charge of US ground forces. Eisenhower, Montgomery, and the SHAEF staff set about finalizing and fine-tuning the invasion plan, the most massive buildup of men and supplies the world had ever seen.

The final plan was composed of three separate components: sea, air, and ground. First was the massive naval phase, Neptune. This involved the transport of troops and equipment across the English Channel aboard a vast armada of ships. As it crossed the channel, the fleet would separate into eastern and western task forces. The two forces would spread out and attack across a 60-mile (100 km) stretch of French coastline.[1] The eastern force would be made up of British and Canadian troops. It would divide into three smaller units, each of which would land at a separate beach. The beaches were code-named Gold, Juno, and Sword.

The US-commanded western task force would divide in two and attack separately at the beaches code-named Utah and Omaha. A small US Army Ranger force would assault Pointe du Hoc, a cliff

PAS-DE-CALAIS

Hitler and many other German military leaders were convinced an Allied invasion would occur at Pas-de-Calais. This portion of France lies across the Strait of Dover, the narrowest part of the English Channel. Approximately 20 miles (32 km) of water separates England from France there.[2] It was the most logical place for the Allies to cross. Located near Calais were a number of harbors and port facilities. The Germans assumed the Allies would need those facilities to bring ashore adequate men, vehicles, and supplies. As a result, they concentrated their defenses near Calais.

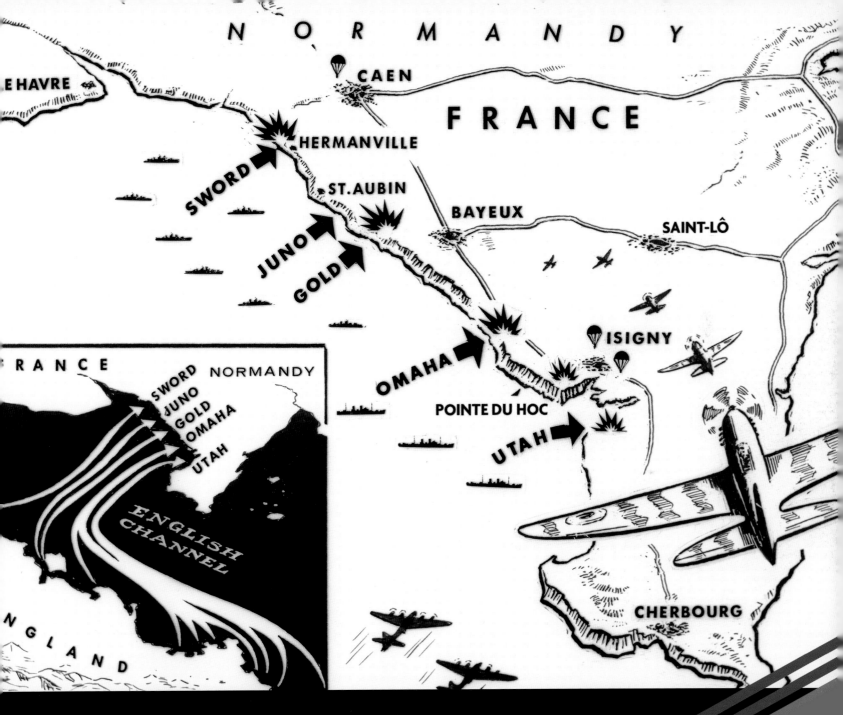

NORMANDY

FRANCE

LE HAVRE

CAEN

HERMANVILLE

SWORD

ST. AUBIN

BAYEUX

SAINT-LÔ

JUNO

GOLD

OMAHA

ISIGNY

POINTE DU HOC

UTAH

CHERBOURG

FRANCE

SWORD NORMANDY
JUNO
GOLD
OMAHA
UTAH

ENGLISH CHANNEL

ENGLAND

The plan for D-Day involved the simultaneous assault of five beaches with tens of thousands of soldiers each, with the goal of overwhelming German defenses.

between the two beaches. A variety of smaller landing craft would transport troops and supplies to the beaches. The giant guns of battleships would fire on German defensive positions both before and during the invasion. After the invasion, British and US ships would provide the Allies with a steady supply of men, weapons, vehicles, and fuel.

The air phase of the invasion involved the preinvasion bombing of German positions and the transport of airborne troops. The goal of the prelanding bombing was to lessen or neutralize German resistance on the beaches.

The night before the landing, gliders and paratroopers would arrive in the Normandy countryside behind the invasion beaches. These soldiers would seize roads and bridges needed for the Allied advance and block German reinforcements from arriving while Allied soldiers on the beaches came ashore and got organized. Fighter planes would engage any German air or ground forces that appeared. Bombers and fighters would continue providing air support to Allied forces after the invasion.

Once ashore and past the threat of German shore defenses, Allied ground troops would organize and begin moving

MINISUBS

Months before D-Day, small British submarines began scouting the French coastline for promising places for the Allied invasion to land. The subs, which carried two to four men, were transported by larger ships to within 50 miles (80 km) of the French coast and lowered into the water.[3] It was a dangerous and uncomfortable mission. The subs were tiny, barely large enough for the men to squeeze into. They cruised unseen along the beaches to examine obstacles and defenses. Divers even left the subs and swam ashore at night for closer looks. They constantly risked detection since they had to surface regularly to renew their air supply.

inland. According to the plan, this would occur by the end of D-Day or shortly thereafter. The main objective would be for the separate landing forces to unite and form a powerful invading army. The combined forces would, as quickly as possible, move out of Normandy and across France. The ultimate goal would be to push the enemy out of France and back to Germany, where the German army would be forced to surrender or be destroyed.

THE BUILDUP

With the Overlord plan in place, events began happening quickly. Through the last months of 1943 and into 1944, the United Kingdom, approximately the size of Colorado, became an enormous military base. Tents and barracks sprang up everywhere. Soldiers marched and trained in the countryside. Public and private spaces—fields, roadsides, yards, gardens, sheds, garages, basements, and even public parks—were stacked and crammed with weapons, ammunition, vehicles, food, clothing, and everything else needed to invade a continent.

Men from every branch of the US and British militaries gathered in ever-increasing numbers to work and train for the big day. By the spring of 1944, there were more than 2 million Americans in the United Kingdom.[4] The drills and maneuvers went on day and night, in good weather and bad. Much of the training involved landing craft. Luckily, the United Kingdom had thousands of miles of coastline, and drilling went on there almost continuously right up to D-Day. Officers drove their men relentlessly. Nothing else mattered more than the initial landing. After all, if attack forces could not get past the obstacles Rommel had placed in their way, no inland battle would even occur.

Allied soldiers trained on British beaches. Real naval artillery barrages were sometimes used to get them used to the feeling of a real battle.

To the men, the repetitive training was harsh. Eisenhower and his officers knew what lay ahead. Very few of the young soldiers did. Many had never been in combat before. The goal of harsh preparation was to make men believe battle would be easy compared to the training. They would find out soon enough it was not. But by that time, their habits and movements would become automatic.

Leaders hoped their troops would perform these actions even in moments of sheer chaos and complete terror.

In April, the final decisions were made. The first week in June, particularly Monday, June 5, and Tuesday, June 6, looked to be ideal for an invasion. Those dates provided a bright moon to help ships and gliders navigate. Rising low tides at dawn on those days would expose German beach obstacles and help landing craft get onto the beaches quickly.

No one thought the master plan was foolproof. Some feared the worst. Churchill privately believed the whole invasion might be doomed to failure. So did Leigh-Mallory. In charge of the airborne phase, he worried men dropped behind German lines would be killed in large numbers. Other officers agreed. Leigh-Mallory begged Eisenhower to cancel the airborne phase of Overlord. His doubts worried Eisenhower, but the invasion's supreme commander believed he had no choice. He knew the air, land, and sea phases had to work together for the invasion to succeed. The plan could not be changed. Eisenhower told members of his military staff, "Every obstacle must be overcome, every inconvenience suffered, and every risk run to ensure that our blow is decisive. We cannot afford to fail."[5]

POSTCARDS FROM NORMANDY

Before the war, the Normandy beaches were a popular destination for British citizens to take summer vacations. Invasion planners asked for any postcards and photos the people of the United Kingdom might have taken there. These images helped planners make the detailed maps and models the Allies needed to prepare for D-Day.

DWIGHT D. EISENHOWER

1890–1969

Just two years before Eisenhower took on the job of supreme commander of the SHAEF, he was almost unknown outside of US military circles. But Ike, as he was known, soon became famous for his organizational and diplomatic skills as commander of Allied forces in North Africa and Europe. Those who served under him recognized his ability to lead and inspire people of many different backgrounds and nationalities and weld them into a unified team. Ike applied a rare combination of down-to-earth charm, quiet intelligence, and high energy to every situation or problem.

By the time Eisenhower took over the daunting task of planning and directing Operation Overlord, he was so well liked even the king of the United Kingdom asked for his autograph. The apparent ease with which Eisenhower made difficult decisions was extraordinary. Many people wondered how he coped with the enormous pressures of orchestrating D-Day.

Eisenhower remained popular after the war. US citizens elected him president in 1952 and again in 1956. After that, he retired and lived in Gettysburg, Pennsylvania, until his death in 1969. Eisenhower is buried at the Eisenhower Presidential Library near his boyhood home in Abilene, Kansas.

To ensure secrecy, no Allied soldiers and only a few officers were told exactly where and when the invasion was going to occur. Still, everyone in the United Kingdom knew something big was about to happen. All the furious training and stockpiling of weapons and materials told them the long-awaited invasion was quickly approaching. Few people were surprised when in the early weeks of May 1944, fighting units were herded into heavily guarded camps enclosed with barbed wire to ensure the invasion plans remained secret.

All remaining training and briefing for the invasion happened inside these cramped spaces. In late May, officers were informed of the final invasion details, and they passed the word on to their men. After this, no one was allowed to leave or contact anyone outside his own compound. More than 175,000 men waited for the big day to arrive.[6]

Troops worked feverishly loading vehicles and equipment into landing craft in

CHAPTER
★ 4 ★

A WAITING GAME

Throughout early 1944, ships sailed from the United States to harbors in England. By May 31, the invasion armada had assembled on the southern coastline of England. The enormous task of loading men and equipment onto the ships and landing craft began. The loading was completed by the morning of June 4.

A key part of the Allied invasion had already begun on May 31 with the work of minesweeper ships. During the previous four years of war, the Allies and the Germans had planted millions of underwater bombs in the English Channel. It was now the job of the specially equipped minesweeper ships to clear safe lanes through the channel for the invasion fleet. The sweepers spread out to open and mark ten separate lanes to France.

There were two lanes each for Neptune's five main assault groups, the US and British task forces scheduled to attack at different beaches along the Normandy coastline. The sweepers completed their slow, dangerous task on June 5. The Germans failed to notice the explosions and naval activity in the channel.

By the morning of June 4, most of the massive invasion fleet had gathered near the Isle of Wight, approximately four miles (6.4 km) off the coast of the United Kingdom. Nearly 3,000 vessels—closer to 5,000 if all the smaller landing craft were counted—waited for the final order for the invasion to begin.[1]

Wind and waves made the wait miserable. Larger ships—destroyers, battleships, and transports—were built for conditions on the open sea. They rode out the stormy weather well. But men aboard smaller landing craft had a much tougher time. These vessels were more like floating boxcars than ships. Making matters worse for the men riding in them was the knowledge they would be among the first to go ashore. That meant their boats would lead the way across the channel. They had to stay in position, ready to go when the order came.

The day wore on and darkness closed in around the fleet. Low clouds swept in, bringing pelting rain. The wind whipped

OPERATION FORTITUDE

The Allies set up a secret project called Operation Fortitude to deceive the Germans by making them think the invasion would not happen at Normandy. Leading up to D-Day, Fortitude agents broadcasted fake radio transmissions to mislead German intelligence officials. They leaked false information to make the Germans believe an invasion might happen at Calais or in Norway. Fortitude workers even created a fictitious army group commanded by famed US lieutenant general George S. Patton. The German army, respecting and fearing Patton, had believed he would lead the eventual invasion. The Allies sent Patton to northern England, where a fake military training camp was set up. They made sure the Germans learned about the camp. This and other ruses led Hitler to believe his hunch about an invasion at Calais was correct.

Soldiers weighed down by full combat gear waited on the choppy waters of the English Channel.

the sea into whitecaps that smacked the landing craft headlong and broadside. The heavily loaded boats plunged deep into wave troughs before rising high on crests. Smaller boats took shelter near larger ships, but the wild bouncing and flinging continued. Cold, soaked, and seasick men huddled in their boats.

THE WEATHER DILEMMA

Inland at command headquarters, Eisenhower knew men were suffering out on the stormy channel. News from Captain J. M. Stagg, the chief British meteorologist, did not make him feel any better. A larger storm system was moving in from the north. Weather for the English Channel was getting worse. The next day looked overcast and rainy with gusting high winds and heavy seas. The bad weather was likely to continue for several days.

This was Eisenhower's worst nightmare. Countless hours of planning, preparation, and training were invested in Overlord. The groundwork was laid. The Allied armies were poised and ready. The fate of Europe depended upon this invasion. It seemed incredible that it all came down to a question of weather. Eisenhower desperately wanted to give the order to invade, yet he knew he could not.

Planes could not fly in such bad weather, and the first phase of the planned invasion was airborne. Troops had to parachute in and secure the countryside behind the invasion beaches. Bombers had to arrive before dawn on D-Day to smash German defenses. Air power was perhaps the Allies' biggest advantage. Without it, a ground invasion had little chance of succeeding. Landing craft and other assault vessels were not built for heavy waves and high wind either. Many probably would not even reach the beaches.

Eisenhower and other key Allied leaders deliberated about the weather before making the final decision to launch the invasion.

To cancel the invasion now would be a catastrophe. But to send it to certain failure would be even worse. Hoping for some sort of weather miracle, Eisenhower put Overlord on hold. He ordered ships to stand by and Stagg to continue monitoring the weather. They would meet the next day, and Eisenhower would make the final decision then.

THE STORM CLEARS

Ships and boats close to land took shelter in harbors and inlets. But most were too far from shore to allow such a maneuver. They spent the night at sea, steering in circles near the Isle of Wight, waiting for further orders. Captains worried they would run out of fuel before a final decision was made. But for the majority of men aboard the vessels, the day was an endless misery of shivering, vomiting, praying, and wondering. The worst thing, most said later, was simply not knowing what was going to happen.

Late in the evening of June 4, 1944, Eisenhower met with his staff again. This time Stagg had encouraging news. The storm raging outside showed signs of breaking. The rain would end by morning, followed by approximately 36 hours of clearer weather. It would remain windy in the channel and western France, though planes and ships would have no trouble operating. In Stagg's opinion, the invasion could take place, but it would be 24 hours behind schedule.

British and US officers cheered the good news. Eisenhower paced, looking worried. The final decision was his. And forecasting the weather, particularly in the North

AIR AND NAVAL SUPREMACY

The Allies had two major advantages over the Germans. By June 1944, Germany's air and naval power had been severely damaged. The Allies had won the Battle of the Atlantic, the struggle to protect Allied shipping from German submarines. This meant US cargo and troop ships could bring much needed help to the United Kingdom. Additionally, the US Eighth and Fifteenth Air Forces and RAF Bomber Command had succeeded in breaking the Luftwaffe fighter force, enabling the Allies to gain air superiority over the continent of Europe. Bombing raids by British and US planes against French railways isolated Normandy from the rest of France.

Atlantic, was always risky. What if Stagg guessed wrong? Thousands of soldiers, pilots, and sailors waited, uncertain of their futures.

Finally, Eisenhower stopped pacing and said, "I am quite positive the order must be given."[2] That was all British Admiral Bertram Ramsay needed to hear. He rushed from the room to send word for the invasion fleet to assemble once again. Weather permitting, the armada would set out during the night of June 5 and arrive off the coast of Normandy in the early morning darkness of June 6. The only remaining action was for Eisenhower to give the final order to launch the invasion.

CHAPTER
★ 5 ★

THE ASSAULT BEGINS

In the early morning hours of June 5, the weather was still windy and rainy. Stagg assured Eisenhower a break would come soon, but Eisenhower hesitated to give the final order. Too much was at stake to make an error now. Stagg thought bad weather could return on June 7 and 8. Eisenhower worried the first waves of troops might get ashore, but air support, additional troops, and needed supplies would be delayed by the weather. That would endanger the entire operation. The general listened to opinions from British and US officers. In the end, though, Eisenhower knew he had to make the final call himself.

Eisenhower later said another thing weighing heavily on his mind was the fact the Germans still did not know when or where the attack was coming. To that point, bad weather had helped the Allies by keeping German scout planes on the ground. As soon as the skies cleared, the Germans would spot the enormous fleet forming in the channel. The element of surprise would be lost, and German forces would rush to meet the invasion.

Eisenhower paced and thought about what to do. Finally, he gave the order. With that, officers scattered in every direction. Moments later, Eisenhower was alone in the room. The invasion was on, but whatever happened now was out of his hands.

At more than 100 airfields in the United Kingdom, pilots and soldiers boarded planes. The first phase of Overlord was a massive air assault. Eisenhower went to a nearby airfield to chat with parachutists and pilots as they loaded. Most men could hardly walk and needed help boarding, weighed down by up to 100 pounds (45 kg) of weapons and equipment. The men were confident, though, and they were relieved to be on their way at last. The first planes roared into the night sky

THE ORDER OF THE DAY

For months, Eisenhower had been working on a special message he would issue to the men he commanded on D-Day. On the morning of June 5, 1944, he had his Order of the Day printed and distributed to the 175,000 men about to depart for the invasion. The message reminded the soldiers of their mission's importance:

Soldiers, Sailors, and Airmen of the Allied Expeditionary Force!

You are about to embark upon the Great Crusade, toward which we have striven these many months. The eyes of the world are upon you. The hopes and prayers of liberty-loving people everywhere march with you. . . .

Your task will not be an easy one. Your enemy is well trained, well equipped, and battle-hardened. He will fight savagely. . . .

I have full confidence in your courage, devotion to duty and skill in battle. We will accept nothing less than full Victory![1]

Eisenhower spoke with the airborne assault troops just before they boarded their aircraft.

at 11:00 p.m.[2] A reporter with Eisenhower noticed the general had tears in his eyes as the last plane disappeared into the darkness.

NIGHT DROP

It took hundreds of C-47 transport aircraft, commonly known as Dakotas, to carry the US 101st and Eighty-Second Airborne Divisions into Normandy. A total of 13,400 US and 7,000 British paratroopers flew into battle.[3]

The first airborne troops to land in France were the pathfinders. These specially trained men parachuted in an hour before the main body of troops arrived. Their job was to set up lights and special radio systems in fields to guide incoming planes to the right landing sites. But of the 18 pathfinder units, only one actually landed in the correct place.

For the men who followed the pathfinders, it was a nerve-wracking approach. Pilots were forbidden to use their radios in case the enemy might be listening. They kept their eyes on a lighted blue dot on the tail of the plane ahead of them in order to maintain their positions. Midair collisions were a constant danger. The planes flew low, only 500 feet (150 m) above the waves in the channel. When they reached the French coast, the planes were suddenly engulfed in thick clouds. Having only a small visual connection to the plane ahead of them, and knowing many more planes were behind them, some pilots panicked. They climbed and veered off in various directions. When they emerged from the clouds minutes later, the planes were widely separated and off course.

Then, German antiaircraft guns opened fire from the ground. The planes bobbed, twisted, and turned to avoid the fire. That took them even further from their original target drop zones. Men preparing to jump were thrown around inside the planes. Jagged fragments of exploded metal and bullets filled the sky and ripped into many planes.

Men had to jump anyway. Many were flying lower and faster than usual as their aircraft reached 150 miles per hour (241 kmh) rather than the expected 90 miles per hour (140 kmh). The pilots sped up to reduce the risk of being hit by ground fire. Others soared to 1,000 feet (300 m) or higher, much higher than most paratroopers had ever jumped even in perfect daylight conditions.[4] Some planes were hit and crashed. Faced with conditions they had never seen or trained for, a few men simply refused to jump. They chose to face military trials and charges of cowardice instead.

But most men jumped. Many troopers later described the terror of descending through webs of glowing tracer bullets and whizzing shrapnel. All around them they saw other troopers plummeting to their deaths, their parachutes ripped apart by flak and machine-gun fire. Some were killed or wounded before they hit the ground.

Paratroopers had little control over where they landed. Many landed badly on rough, uneven ground and suffered broken bones. Some fell into trees or

DUMMY PARACHUTISTS

To draw attention away from the real airborne assault, one British unit staged a fake attack. They dropped 500 cloth and wooden dummies in the countryside miles from the actual drop zone.[5] Each dummy was rigged with a small explosive charge that went off when it hit the ground. Several real men jumped with the fake ones. On the ground, they fired guns and played loud recordings of troops assembling and fighting, drawing thousands of German defenders away from Allied landing zones and the invasion beaches.

Paratroopers lined up inside their aircraft and jumped in rapid succession.

water, onto rooftops, or even onto busy city streets. One man landed so far off target he wandered around alone for five days without seeing anyone. Another trooper's parachute became snagged on a church steeple in the village of Sainte-Mère-Église. US Army private John Steele dangled there, playing dead above the town for two hours before German soldiers took him prisoner.

CONFUSION AND DISORDER

Despite the hazards, most paratroopers managed to float down safely, though they had been somewhat dazed and awed by their first taste of combat. When they landed, few were able to find their units. The wind and the wild turning and veering of the planes' paths had scattered jumpers randomly all over the countryside.

CRICKETS IN THE DARK

Each parachutist was given a small toy known as a cricket that made a loud clicking sound. Airborne soldiers were told to click once and wait for a two-click response. Any other movement or sound in the dark was to be considered hostile.

The stories the troopers later told were similar for most units. They had no idea where they were. The men they were supposed to link up and fight with could not be found. Invasion organizers had decided against using radios for the same reason planes did not use them—so they could remain undetected by the enemy.

Soldiers began joining any group they could find. Using crickets, tiny metal devices that made clicking noises, they were able to identify fellow invaders in the darkness. Others simply called out to fellow troops. Many wandered around confused in the blackness looking for groups to join. They began forming improvised fighting units. Whenever officers could gather enough men, they began moving toward whatever mission their unit had been assigned. That meant as night wore on, more and more men became part of missions they had not trained for.

In some ways, the confusion and disarray of the Allied units had a positive effect on the assault. The German defenders were just as confused. They could not tell if stray Allied soldiers were part of a mixed-up raid or something much bigger.

The French Resistance added to the confusion. These loosely organized, roving groups of ordinary French citizens and more seasoned fighters worked to disrupt German efforts and assist the Allies. Both paratroopers and the Resistance members cut telephone lines all over Normandy. At crucial moments, the Germans found they could not contact commanders or other units.

The way the German chain of command was set up compounded problems. German officers needed permission from higher-ranking commanders to move reinforcements to Normandy. To move the armored reserves near Paris required permission directly from Adolf Hitler. It took a great deal of time and trouble to go through all those levels of command.

Divisions of Panzers, or tanks, were particularly vital to the Germans. With fighter planes mostly unavailable, tanks were their most powerful and mobile weapons. In fact, the 125th regiment of the German Twenty-First Panzer Division at Caen was ready to go, yet it could not move. It needed direct permission from Hitler, who could not be reached. As far away as Paris, German commanders were getting scattered, confused messages. They could not tell what was happening.

By 3:00 a.m., Allied gliders began landing with troops, guns, and jeeps. They did a little better than the paratroopers. In one area, nearly 50 of 70 gliders landed safely, bringing to land a regiment of the Sixth Airborne Division.[6] Still, others crashed in the hedgerow country. Some came down in low areas flooded by Rommel's defenders. Many men and their equipment were lost, and only a few companies were able to assemble and find the gear and weapons they needed to complete their missions. By 4:00 a.m., paratroopers and glider troopers were scattered all over the Cotentin Peninsula. Very few were where they were supposed to be. Most could not attack assigned targets because so much equipment—including maps and weapons—had been lost in botched landings.

NATURAL OBSTACLES: HEDGEROWS

Bushes proved to be one of the most challenging problems the Allies had to overcome in France. These natural fences have divided fields and lined roads in Normandy for centuries. Preinvasion planners and trainers failed to realize the gnarled shrubs and small trees stood atop dirt mounds 12 feet (3.6 m) high, much taller and thicker than hedgerows in England.[7] As a result, paratroopers fumbled and struggled through thick growth, and many gliders slammed into bushes in the darkness.

Yet slowly, despite the difficulties, some fighting units assembled and moved into position. Small, mismatched groups connected and achieved some successes. Before dawn on D-Day, airborne troops cut important communication lines. They seized and held key bridges, and they destroyed German military posts. The plan of confusing and distracting the Germans from the beach invasions coming at dawn had largely worked.

The key village Sainte-Mère-Église, located on an important road, was secured. But objectives to seize other villages and secure exits behind Utah Beach went unfulfilled. At dawn, many men were still mostly lost and scattered in the countryside beyond the coast. To make matters worse, the German Sixth

Paratroopers worked to secure key areas behind enemy lines in preparation for the beach landings.

Parachute Division, one of Hitler's best, was on its way. This well-trained unit was made up of 3,500 seasoned German soldiers.[8] They were tough and mobile and among the first in Normandy on D-Day to receive permission to form a counterattack. They had no air or tank support and no large weapons. Yet they were supremely confident they could defeat any Allied unit they might face.

ERWIN ROMMEL

1891–1944

General Erwin Rommel was a German national hero and Hitler's personal favorite general. As the cunning and creative commander of Hitler's Afrika Korps, Rommel was given the nickname "The Desert Fox" by Allied troops.

By the time Hitler put him in charge of the Atlantic Wall defenses in November 1943, Rommel had been promoted to field marshal. Rommel began his command with an inspection of the many individual fortifications built to protect the coast of Europe. He found they were not nearly strong enough to repel an Allied invasion. "Our only possible chance will be at the beaches," he said. "That is where the enemy is always weakest."[9] He supervised massive improvements and additions. It soon became clear, however, that concrete defenses and huge guns alone would not stop an invasion. Rommel insisted large numbers of troops and tanks must be in place behind the shore installations.

The Normandy invasion was Rommel's final battle. He was severely wounded by an air strike after D-Day but survived. As he recovered, he became convinced Hitler needed to be replaced and began to associate himself with a plot to assassinate the German leader. Hitler discovered his field marshal's betrayal and forced him to commit suicide with poison on October 14, 1944. The German public was told Rommel had died from his wounds, and he was given a hero's funeral.

The story of Rommel's death remained largely secret until after the war. Today, he is widely regarded as a brilliant tactician and military commander.

THE FLEET ARRIVES

All night, while the paratroopers struggled to get their bearings, the wind-whipped Allied fleet plowed slowly across the English Channel. The slowest type of boat was the heavily loaded Landing Ship, Tank (LST). These vitally important landing craft were designed specifically to deposit men, machinery, weapons, and supplies directly onto dry land. Some LSTs towed Rhino ferries, too. These flat-bottomed barges were loaded with even more trucks, bulldozers, jeeps, and other equipment. The rest of the ships transported men and smaller landing craft.

The first ships arrived approximately 11 miles (18 km) off the French coast at 2:00 a.m. The Germans still had not detected the mass of ships bearing down on them. An hour later, though, one radar station finally spotted the fleet. Shore batteries were alerted and several small boats were sent to investigate.

The rest of the armada arrived between 2:00 and 4:00 a.m. The ships spread out and formed five battle groups. Like five sharp prongs at the end of a spear, they would strike at the same time at different beaches across nearly 60 miles (100 km) of Normandy coastline. From east to west, the beaches were code-named Sword, Juno, Gold, Omaha, and Utah. British and Canadian troops would storm Sword, Juno, and Gold. The US forces would attack Omaha and Utah.

All along the Normandy coast, troop transport ships took their assigned positions. Crews began lowering small landing craft known as Higgins boats into the water. They draped wide mesh nets over the sides of the transport ships so men could climb down to board the Higgins boats. In the predawn darkness, with ships heaving and rolling wildly, seasick men overloaded with equipment and weapons had a hard time getting over the sides of the transport ships. The climb down to the landing craft 20 feet (6 m) below was an even tougher challenge. The small, light landing craft bobbed like corks on passing swells, rising and falling by as much as ten feet (3 m). Soldiers struggled

FOILING THE ENEMY

Before D-Day, Allied bombers had done an excellent job destroying German radar sites along the French coast, but they could not destroy them all. So ahead of the invasion fleet, Allied planes dropped hundreds of pounds of foil strips that fluttered and floated on the wind. Radar beams bounced off this swirling metallic curtain, masking the approach of the invasion force. The trick created all sorts of confusing, false echoes on German radar screens. It also created the impression that the target of the invasion fleet was Pas-de-Calais, far to the north of the Normandy landing site.

THE GREATEST SHOW EVER STAGED

The Allied air forces had more than 10,000 planes in the skies over Normandy on D-Day. Approximately half were fighter planes, which had very little to do.[2] No real opposition had been expected, since Germany's battered air force lacked the strength to challenge the Allied fighters. Still, planners wanted Allied air power in place just in case it was needed.

US and British aerial firepower could have been used to good advantage against German ground forces. But Allied air and ground forces had not yet created effective means to communicate with each other. So fighter pilots simply circled overhead, watching the battle unfolding beneath them. One of them later called it "the greatest show ever staged."[3]

to hang on to the nets. They had to time their hop down to the landing craft for the moment when the boats were at the top of a wave.

Each Higgins boat carried up to 30 men and their assorted gear. In most cases, there was no room to sit down or turn around. As each boat finished loading, the coxswain, or boat pilot, steered it away into the darkness and began circling, waiting for the rest of the landing flotilla to form.

On the landing craft, seasickness became a greater problem. Earlier, on the large transport ships, vomit bags had been provided. On the Higgins boats, there were none. For most men the sides of the boat were at eyelevel, so there was no way to lean over the side. The misery of those pre-dawn hours, trapped in a tiny boat with dozens of vomiting men, would remain an enduring D-Day memory for many veterans.

At first light, approximately 5:20 a.m., 1,200 bombers of the US Eighth and Ninth Air Forces swept in.[1] For the next half-hour, flying only 500 to 1,000 feet (150–300 m) over the beaches, the bombers targeted German shore batteries and defenses. At the same time, high-altitude bombers dropped bombs that unfortunately landed inland beyond the range of German shore defenses.

Many pilots and crews were hesitant to drop bombs blindly, not knowing exactly where they might fall. They knew airborne troops had landed hours earlier and were moving to positions in the countryside below. Some of those units could be quite close to the beach defenses. Also, large numbers of landing craft were approaching the beaches from the sea. Strong winds, ground fire, and bomb blasts buffeted the low-flying planes. Fear of hitting their own men forced some pilots to halt bombing altogether.

One main objective of the bombardment was to stun and terrify the defenders. According to some German soldiers who survived D-Day to tell their stories later, it certainly did that. The bombardment was also intended to provide deep holes where landing soldiers could take shelter later. It accomplished this task better at some beaches than others. In some areas, the bombs made craters on top of overlooking bluffs rather than below them, where they were more desperately needed. Still, the sight of the bombing made hundreds of men watching from landing craft feel a little better.

Destroyers and battleships began their bombardment at 5:50 a.m. The thunderous firing from large ships nearly deafened the men on the small landing boats circling around them. Everyone felt the concussions as massive guns launched shell after shell at the shore. Men watched gigantic shells soar over their heads, forming fountains of flame and towers of smoke when they hit their targets and exploded. Soon the entire shoreline was engulfed in smoke.

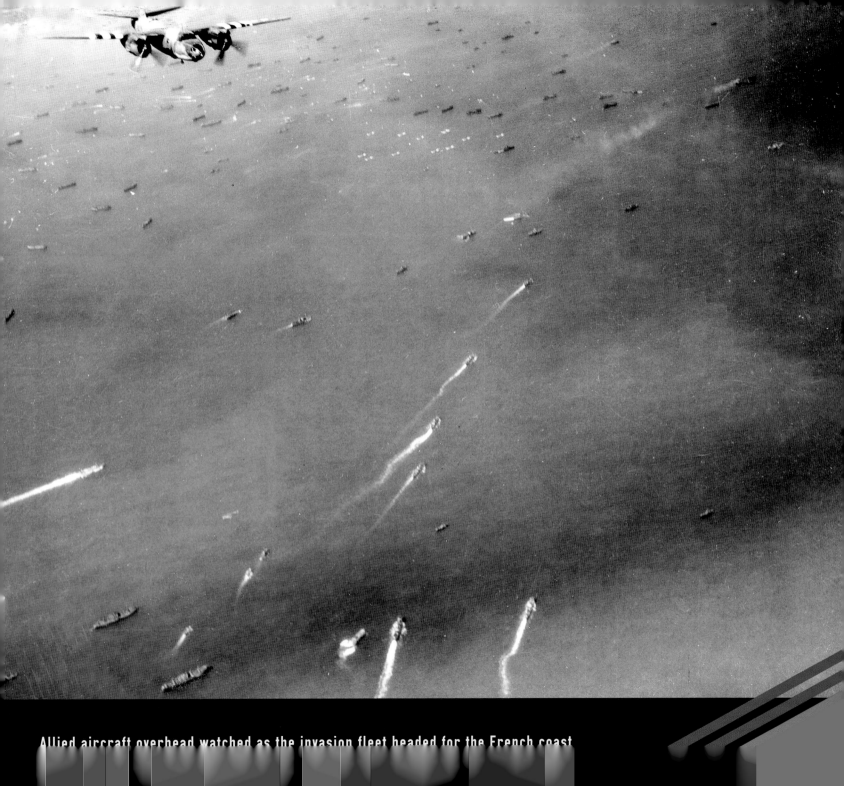

Allied aircraft overhead watched as the invasion fleet headed for the French coast

The battleship _Nevada_ was among the Allied vessels bombarding the beach defenses.

Wind quickly cleared the smokescreen, and German guns began firing at the invasion force. Men in Higgins boats, drawing ever closer to the shore, felt like sitting ducks. The larger Allied ships moved along behind the slowly advancing landing craft, firing over their heads. The ships concentrated fire on areas picked out days or weeks earlier—bunkers, pillboxes, casemates and gun installations. Allied spotters on the ships watched for flashes and puffs of smoke on shore, revealing the positions of German guns. They directed fire at those points.

Finally, as the first landing vessels neared the shore, the naval bombardment stopped. Despite repeated direct hits on many targets, Allied reports would later show the bombardment did little damage to the German defenses. Rommel and his builders had poured thousands of tons of concrete. The Atlantic Wall had withstood the worst attack modern weapons could throw at it. The men about to land in the first waves on Normandy beaches would soon find the German troops were ready to fiercely defend the shoreline.

LANDING CRAFT

Everything on D-Day depended upon soldiers and equipment getting ashore as quickly as possible. Special kinds of vessels were needed to accomplish that task.

LANDING CRAFT, INFANTRY (LCI)

The LCI was a boat approximately 160 feet (50 m) long that could carry up to 200 soldiers and their equipment. Many men made the long, miserable trip across the English Channel in these vessels. Ramps in front dropped down to allow men to unload quickly.

LANDING CRAFT, TANK (LCT)

The LCT was approximately 120 feet (37 m) long. It could carry several tanks or trucks, plus crewmembers.

LANDING SHIP, TANK (LST)

The LST proved crucial on D-Day and in the days, weeks, and months after the invasion. In fact, the invasion was postponed from May to June 1944 to allow for more of these key vessels to be constructed. The large, flat-bottomed ships could deposit troops, tanks, and vehicles directly onto the shore. More than 230 LSTs delivered huge volumes of equipment and supplies ashore on and after D-Day. They also served as hospital ships that evacuated dead and wounded soldiers to the United Kingdom.

Soldiers at the US beaches poured out of Higgins boats, waded through the surf, and searched for cover from incoming bullets and shells.

THE AMERICAN BEACHES

Attacks began at 6:30 a.m. on the two US beaches, Utah and Omaha. Utah, the westernmost of all five D-Day beaches, was approximately 11 miles (18 km) long. Directly to the east was Omaha, a crescent-shaped beach approximately 9 miles (14 km) long. Omaha was approximately 300 to 400 yards (270 to 370 m) deep from the water to the cliffs at low tide. At high tide it shrank to just 10 to 20 yards (9 to 18 m). An inlet and muddy tidal flat at the mouth of the Vire River separated the two beaches. The US Army's Fourth Infantry Division assaulted Utah, while the First and Twenty-ninth Infantry Divisions led the way ashore at Omaha.

At both beaches, LCTs were supposed to be the first Allied craft to approach shore. These craft carried amphibious tanks. The tanks were designed to be launched more than one mile (1.6 km) from shore and propel themselves to the beaches. They were meant to provide cover for the waves of US soldiers coming ashore in Higgins boats and other landing craft.

UTAH BEACH

At Utah, strong currents and wind drove Higgins boats off course. Many arrived approximately one-half mile (0.8 km) east of the point where they were supposed to land. The error caused a great deal of confusion at first. Soldiers hitting the beaches did not recognize the terrain or the specific positions they had trained to attack.

The mistake worked in their favor. The strongest German defenses at Utah turned out to be closer to the original landing point. So, although the US troops were technically in the wrong place, they faced lighter enemy resistance during the landing than they might otherwise have expected. Additionally, Utah was the only beach where the preinvasion bombing had accomplished anything meaningful. Through the skill of the bomber pilots who targeted the German emplacements on the beach, a concrete fortress and its large guns adjacent to Utah had been destroyed. With only smaller weapons available to oppose the immense onslaught approaching from the sea, German

WHILE HITLER SLEPT

On D-Day, Hitler failed to order reinforcements to Normandy until it was too late. Some people reported later he liked to sleep late and that no one was willing to risk waking him early on June 6 to tell him about the invasion. The more likely reason for the delay was that neither Hitler nor his generals could decide if the Normandy invasion was the real one or a deception. By the time they decided to take action, the Allies already had a solid foothold in Europe.

Troops on Utah Beach soon cleared out the German defenses and began moving inland toward their objectives.

resistance quickly crumbled. Approximately 600 Allied men became casualties at Utah.[1] Despite these losses, the invasion at Utah Beach was nearly perfect.

By 9:00 a.m., the amphibious tanks had arrived and the next waves of landing craft began sweeping ashore. The beach quickly backed up in an enormous traffic jam of men and vehicles, as soldiers and engineers worked frantically to clear exits and get men and machines rolling inland. Commanders knew the success at Utah would mean nothing if they could not get their army away from the ocean to the interior of Normandy. Within a few hours engineers and bulldozers succeeded in constructing roadways off the beach, and men and vehicles began pouring inland. The way was now clear for US forces to move west to take the city of Cherbourg and east to link up with other US and British units.

TEDDY ROOSEVELT LEADS THE CHARGE

Brigadier General Teddy Roosevelt Jr. was the son of former president Theodore Roosevelt, who led a force of soldiers nicknamed the "Rough Riders" up San Juan Hill in Cuba during the Spanish-American War (1898). At 56 years old, Teddy Jr. was the oldest man and the only general to go ashore on D-Day. Roosevelt led soldiers ashore in the first wave at Utah Beach. He received the Medal of Honor for his extraordinary courage under fire, but died several weeks later of a heart attack.

"A SHOOTING GALLERY"

Conditions at Omaha Beach, approximately 20 miles (32 km) to the east, were much worse. Amphibious tanks that rolled off landing craft three miles (5 km) from shore floundered in the heavy waves. Tank after tank drove off the lowered ramps of the LCTs and simply sank in deep water. Their floatation devices were unable to keep the large waves from swamping the vehicles. Of the 34 tanks first launched off Omaha Beach, only five eventually made it ashore. Some tank crews were unable to get out in time and drowned.

German defenses were far stronger and more numerous at Omaha than at any of the other beaches. Germans guns there had been virtually untouched by the air and naval bombardment, which was too short and unfocused to have much of an effect on enemy installations. The volume and accuracy of enemy fire was stunning to the soldiers aboard the incoming landing craft. German shelling and mines blasted some of the Higgins boats even before they reached the shore.

Obstacles, sandbars, and tidal currents interfered with many landing craft far from shore. Snagged, unable to move forward, some of the landing vessel drivers dropped the steel ramps before they reached shore. Men, weighed down with equipment and weapons, rushed off and immediately sank in deep water. Some drowned, while others were able to shed heavy guns and packs and bob their way ashore. They waded hundreds of feet before reaching the beach—exhausted, unarmed, and helpless. All the while, German guns, large and small, fired from multiple angles.

With no cover aside from beach obstacles and a few shell craters, the first waves of soldiers who made it to the beach faced the full force of enemy fire. In front of them lay a long stretch of wet sand and a ferocious crisscross pattern of machine-gun fire. Above and from all sides, large artillery pieces in concrete casemates zeroed in on the landing zone. Nearby bluffs—rugged, 100-foot (30 m) cliffs rimming the beach—were studded with underground tunnels connecting dozens of large and small firing points. Defenders inside the tunnels could move around unseen, while attackers on the beach had no place to hide. One company from the Twenty-ninth Infantry Division lost 96 percent of its men in the first moments on Omaha.[2] A soldier later recalled the beach as "a shooting gallery." Another said simply, "I became a visitor to hell."[3]

Many of those who somehow managed to survive the first gruesome hour on Omaha Beach believed the massive assault had been a miserable failure.

HIGGINS BOATS

Without the Higgins boats, most experts agree, the outcome of the D-Day invasion of Normandy may have been very different. The boats were named for Andrew Jackson Higgins. He owned and operated Higgins Industries, a private company in New Orleans, Louisiana. When he learned of the US military's urgent need for a sturdy landing boat, he designed and built one based on the flat-bottomed boats used in the oil industry in Louisiana.

Higgins Industries repeatedly set records for production of military boats and ships. In 1943 alone, in preparation for D-Day, Higgins's eight plants produced more landing craft than all other shipyards in the nation combined. By September of that year, 12,964 of the US Navy's 14,072 vessels were products of Higgins Industries.[4]

In addition to their service in Normandy, Higgins boats were used in the Pacific war against Japan. Historians agree that without these little boats, beach landings would have been much harder and casualties significantly higher. Allied leaders also recognized the importance of Higgins's landing craft. Eisenhower later called Andrew Higgins "the man who won the war for us."[5]

Troops whose Higgins boats sank offshore were helped to the beach by fellow soldiers.

In despair, wounded and terrified men crouched behind jagged obstacles, the burning hulks of tanks, and even the bodies of their fallen comrades. Survival became their only objective.

RANGERS AT POINTE DU HOC

US Army Rangers were sent to knock out six large-caliber German guns at the highest point overlooking Omaha and Utah Beaches, Pointe du Hoc. To reach the installation, the Rangers launched rocket-propelled grappling hooks to the top of the cliff. Then they scaled the sheer, 100-foot (30 m) cliffs on ropes while under fire from above. When they arrived at the top, they found the six guns had been moved inland. But the soldiers soon found the guns and tons of ammunition nearby and destroyed them. German counterattacks nearly destroyed the Ranger force. By the end of the fighting, only 90 of 200 Rangers were unwounded.[6] Yet, they repelled repeated German attempts to retake Pointe du Hoc until relieved by US troops arriving overland from Omaha Beach two days later.

It soon became clear to many men that the only way to stay alive was to somehow make it to the base of the steep bluff at the back of the beach. The German guns could not hit this area. To get there, however, soldiers had to cross a flat, gravelly area randomly strewn with mines and backed by a vicious snarl of barbed wire. These obstacles had to be blasted out for the men to pass. But many of them had lost their gear, including weapons and explosives, just getting ashore.

The next waves of Allied landing craft began arriving. Through the smoke and haze, officers could see the first wave of soldiers at Omaha was bogged down and in serious trouble. It seemed they could be on the verge of being completely wiped out. The beach was strewn with dead and wounded soldiers and piles of weapons and equipment. Gullies and depressions in the steep bluffs all around had to be blasted open and bulldozed before anything or anyone could get off the beach. This was already happening at Utah and other beaches, but it could not happen at Omaha until German artillery and machine guns had been silenced.

GETTING OFF THE BEACH

New arrivals joined the few exhausted, bewildered soldiers at the back of the beach. Some brought explosives and blew holes in the barbed-wire obstacles. This allowed men to make it to relative safety at the base of the bluffs. There, strung out along the nine-mile (14 km) length of beach, dazed individuals and groups huddled for cover. Medics struggled to treat and evacuate their severely wounded comrades.

At approximately 7:45 a.m., a few soldiers made a sudden, critical decision. It became clear they had to get off the beach to survive, and the only way off was up. The soldiers began to climb the bluffs overlooking Omaha Beach. When they encountered bunkers and enemy positions, they blasted them with hand grenades or fired into them with rifles.

All along the beach, men seemed to come to the same conclusion. Unaware others were also climbing, they began a slow, dangerous ascent. Soldiers who had not trained together, and in most cases had never even met, formed small assault groups and attacked instead of waiting to be killed. A few units managed to land on the beach intact, and these groups had a major impact on the struggle to get off the beach.

When reinforceme... beach defenders.

With no real support or direction, in single-file lines, soldiers crept slowly up the steep hillside, pausing to blast German defenses whenever they could. The goal became reaching the top of the bluff. As German positions began falling, one by one, defenders shifted around inside their network of tunnels. Arriving Allied units took advantage of momentary pauses in German firing and made it safely across the beach. Fresh troops and weapons added much-needed support to those who were climbing and fighting.

Destroyer captains saw the desperate upward movement on the shore and moved in, sometimes dangerously close, to support it. They began blasting away at German positions. Spotters on the ships directed fire to cover the infantry advance. Launching five-inch (13 cm) shells at close range directly into pillboxes and bunkers accomplished what random shelling had not done earlier. The support energized the soldiers and encouraged more of them to advance. Many of the men on the beach that day later credited the risky action taken by Allied ships as saving the day at Omaha.

By 9:30 a.m., commanders offshore began to spot Allied soldiers rallying on the top crest of the bluff. After that, the momentum of the battle began favoring the Allies. Once they were above the beach and out of direct fire from the heaviest German guns, scattered handfuls of soldiers rejoined and launched coordinated assaults on enemy positions. German defenders felt the shift, too, and many began surrendering. They had discovered what Rommel had stated earlier: the Atlantic Wall was of no use once the Allies broke through it. With German guns focused on the beaches, the defenders had counted on pushing the

invasion force back into the sea. Once the Allies advanced inland, there was no way to stop them.

By nightfall, US soldiers had established a narrow beachhead at Omaha. The beach was secure, but any German counterattack the next day could have been disastrous. However, the success at the other beaches, the movement of troops inland, and the total Allied air superiority did not allow that to happen. In the days following D-Day, the arrival of more reinforcements and tanks strengthened Omaha and opened exits from the beach.

Casualties overall were far fewer than D-Day planners had estimated. That did not take away the horror of the slaughter at Omaha Beach. One estimate suggests 3,686 men were killed or wounded there on June 6.[7] This represents more than the total number who fell at the three British beaches combined.

In the end, planning and strategy played only a minor role in the final outcome at Omaha. Analyzing the battle in hindsight, most military experts have concluded that success relied on the bravery and determination of individual soldiers. These men improvised, adapted to

BEACHMASTERS

One of the Allies' keys to success on D-Day was logistics—their plans for getting supplies quickly to the people who need them most. On the Normandy beaches, this was accomplished by beachmasters. Every D-Day beach was divided into several sectors, or zones, and each sector had its own beachmaster. Even under enemy fire, these soldiers directed traffic, supervised unloading, and brought order to the chaos of the invasion. Beachmasters were like traffic police. On the beaches they had absolute authority, regardless of their actual rank. Even a general had to wait his turn if the beachmaster said so.

Troops and equipment poured ashore once the beaches were secure.

the changing situation, and overcame overwhelming odds to secure a foothold in France and begin the long-awaited liberation of Europe from Nazi tyranny.

JUNO, SWORD, AND GOLD

While US troops battled on the western beaches, British and Canadian troops were engaged in equally dramatic action to the east. At Juno, Sword, and Gold, the initial conditions and obstacles were comparable to those at the US landing sites. Nearly half of the landing craft at Juno were damaged coming ashore, and a quarter sank.[1] Casualties among first-wave troops at the eastern beaches were just as bad as at Omaha.

As bad as it was in the first hour, however, things improved rapidly after that. One reason for this was that more tanks reached the shore earlier than at Omaha. Also, there were no steep, rugged bluffs at the eastern beaches. Bunkers and guns were easier to approach and attack. German defenders were not as deeply entrenched in as many hidden holes and tunnels as they were at the

US beaches. Resort towns with fine vacation hotels and homes overlooked Juno, Sword, and Gold.

As Allied troops stormed defenses and moved off Juno, Sword, and Gold Beaches, they generally found the enemy less willing and able than the defenders at Omaha. The soldiers they encountered were often quite young or old, and some were even disabled veterans. Many were from German-occupied nations, such as the Soviet Union and Poland. They had relatively little allegiance to Hitler and Germany. Having been forced into service, they were often eager to surrender.

BAGPIPERS

Scottish bagpipers were seen and heard aboard British and Canadian ships during the English Channel crossing. The tradition of bagpipers leading troops into battle is an old and honored one. The pipers were ordered not to go ashore, but many went anyway. One of them, Scotland's Bill Millin, waded into the water at Juno Beach holding his bagpipes over his head. He continued playing even during the worst fighting. He survived the invasion and the war, living to the age of 88.

MOVING INLAND

There were no hedgerows in the country behind the three eastern beaches. Once inland, Canadian and British forces moved rapidly toward their objectives, which included airports, crossroads, and key towns and villages. Combined British-Canadian efforts at Juno brought ashore 900 tanks, hundreds of large field guns, and more than 4,000 short tons (3,600 metric tons) of supplies.[2] The Canadians alone suffered approximately 1,200 casualties at Juno Beach.[3] At Gold and Sword, the British suffered approximately 2,300 casualties.[4]

German prisoners were marched to the shoreline, where ships would take them to

After the disaster at Dieppe two years earlier, Canadian divisions found their success at Juno Beach particularly satisfying. In fact, Canadians made it farther into France than any other Allied force on D-Day.

HOBART'S FUNNIES

British Major General Percy Hobart devised a number of odd-looking but highly effective inventions that became known as Hobart's Funnies. His amphibious tank, known as a DD tank, was used on D-Day. Some soldiers referred to it as the Donald Duck tank. It was a standard Sherman tank that could float inside an inflatable canvas collar or screen. It had propellers that moved it forward in water. On shore, the canvas flotation collar was removed and the DD moved on tracks like any other tank. Hobart also designed a tank that could easily and quickly lay down a short bridge. Another had a large spinning drum in front. Chains attached to the drum beat the ground ahead of the tank, setting off mines. Yet another tank carried a huge fuel tank in back that allowed its gun to shoot out streams of flame.

The same traffic jam of men, vehicles, and supplies happening on the US beaches was found on the British and Canadian beaches. People and equipment tried to squeeze off the beaches through narrow exits. It took time for a steady flow to begin moving inland. Forward units had to hold back the enemy for as long as possible to allow support to come.

The Germans made one attempt at a counterattack against the D-Day invasion. At 4:00 p.m., tanks from the 21st Panzer division staged an attack from Caen against British and Canadian forces moving inland from Sword Beach. These were among the best tanks and warriors the Germans had. But the British and Canadians had managed to bring ashore a supply of antitank weapons. Allied aircraft joined in the fight, too, and one by one the German tanks and their associated

Heavy Allied bombing of the Pas-de-Calais led the Germans to believe an attack might

infantry units were destroyed. The counterattack failed. At the end of the day, most of Hitler's mighty tanks were still far to the north, waiting for an invasion at Calais that never came.

MULBERRIES

After D-Day, the Allies desperately needed harbors where men and supplies could be unloaded quickly and in large numbers. They constructed two artificial harbors called Mulberries. These were built by sinking old or prefabricated ships in shallow water just offshore at Omaha and Gold Beaches. Concrete segments built in the United Kingdom were floated to France and assembled as piers. Each Mulberry harbor was two miles (3.2 km) long and one mile (1.6 km) wide. Although a storm soon destroyed the Mulberry in the US zone, an estimated 500,000 men and 80,000 vehicles were unloaded at these man-made ports.[5]

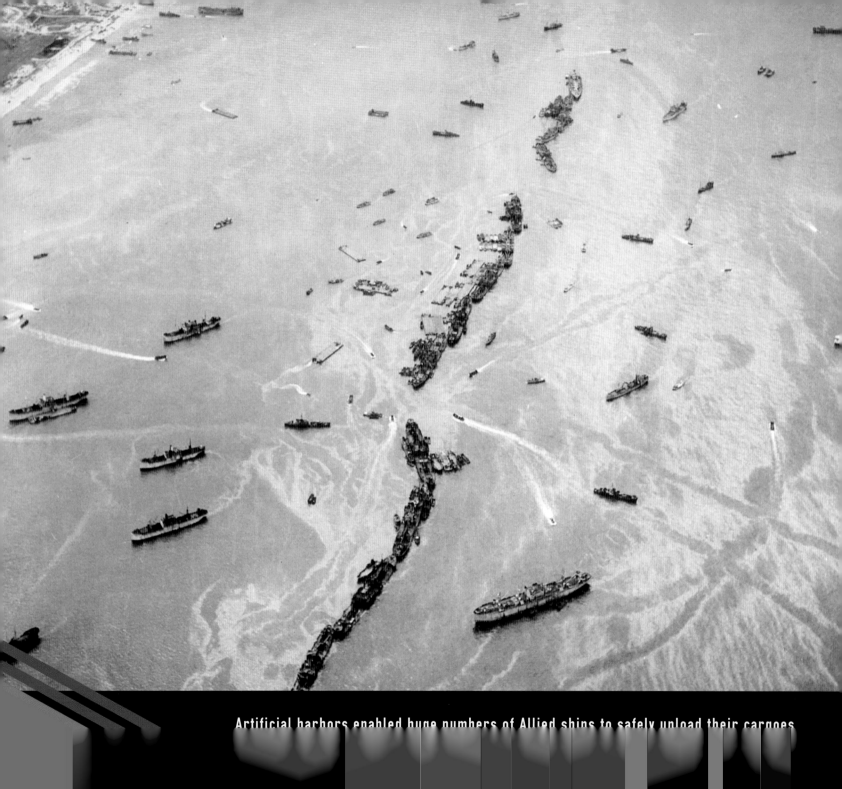

Artificial harbors enabled huge numbers of Allied ships to safely unload their cargoes.

CHAPTER
★ **9** ★

THE ALLIES PREVAIL

The Battle of Normandy did not end with victory on the beaches. Breaking through Hitler's Atlantic Wall was just the first step. By late afternoon on D-Day, the Allied invasion clung to a few miles of French coastline. Only minor holes had been punched through the wall. Now it was urgent to get a flood of men and war machinery flowing across the beaches and into the French countryside. That was where the real Battle of Normandy would be won. The Allied army needed to fight its way out of Normandy and begin a headlong charge toward Germany.

It was several days before the massive traffic jam of men, vehicles, supplies, and equipment at the beaches finally got moving. When it did, it swept forward along routes opened by Allied air power and ground attacks.

In at least one area, the Allied advance hit a snag. In the French countryside, the same thick hedgerows that had wrecked many

HEDGE CUTTERS

US sergeant Curtis Culin helped solve the gnarly problem hedgerows presented. He salvaged jagged steel from piles of destroyed German beach obstacles. He fashioned sharp blades and installed them on the front of his tank. The cutters dug into the tough hedgerows, allowing the tank's engine to plow through the shrubbery. US commanders quickly ordered the installation of the devices on other tanks. Infantry charged through the gaps the tanks cleared, and the Allied advance soon resumed.

gliders now entangled infantry and tanks. The natural barriers proved tougher than any man-made obstacle Rommel's engineers had built. German defenders hunkered down in brush so thick even powerful tanks could not push through. When they tried to climb over the high mounds, tanks got caught in the thick shrubbery, exposing their thinly armored undersides to enemy antitank weapons.

Throughout June, divisions of the First US Army fought through flooded fields and hedgerows, moving toward Cherbourg. With that port secured, US troops headed for the town of Saint-Lô. In late July, Lieutenant General Omar Bradley planned an operation to break out of Normandy. This action, code-named Operation Cobra, was supported by massive air power. It succeeded in breaking the First US Army out of its initial positions in Normandy.

After fierce fighting, in August US and Canadian units approached the town of Falaise, approximately 40 miles (64 km) south of the D-Day beaches. Their advance nearly managed to trap a large number of German troops retreating ahead of them. Approximately 30,000 Germans broke through the gap between the US and Canadian lines and escaped. Still, 50,000 German soldiers were either

Allied tanks and troops moved through bombed-out French cities as they spread out

GERMAN POWS

Thousands of German soldiers surrendered or were captured on D-Day and after. Many were taken back to the invasion beaches and loaded onto ships that took them to camps in the United Kingdom, the United States, and Canada. Thirty-three detention facilities were established in Texas alone. The Allies took 30,000 prisoners every month from D-Day until Christmas 1944.[3]

killed or taken prisoner, and the way was cleared for the vast Allied army still pouring ashore to move out of Normandy.[1]

This ended the Normandy campaign and set the stage for the final Allied offensive across Europe—to Paris, Brussels, the German border, and Hitler's doorstep in Berlin. Hitler committed suicide in his Berlin bunker on April 30, 1945. With US, British, Canadian, and Soviet troops marching through Germany, the Nazi leadership surrendered on Friday, May 8. World War II was over in Europe.

D-DAY IN PERSPECTIVE

The 11-week Battle of Normandy after D-Day proved more successful than almost anyone had dared to hope. Victory came at a steep price, however. It was among the war's deadliest battles in Western Europe.

On June 8, 1944, the Normandy American Cemetery, the first US cemetery established in France during World War II, was built overlooking Omaha Beach. Millions of people have visited it since. On June 6, 2014, veterans and world leaders gathered there and at other D-Day sites to observe the seventieth anniversary of the momentous invasion. French President Francois Hollande described D-Day as "a day that changed the world."[2] US President Barack Obama said the United States' commitment to liberty and freedom "is written in blood on these beaches, and it will endure for eternity."[4]

Veterans of the epic battle can perhaps understand its significance better than most. Over the years, they returned to Normandy in large numbers. As veterans of World War II grew older, fewer and fewer came each year. By the 2010s, most were getting too old to travel any longer. For many, remembering what happened there is painful.

The Allied invasion on D-Day was one of the most critical events of World War II. It was the largest and most complex invasion ever staged. It was also one of the most complicated and difficult feats of military organization and planning ever accomplished.

D-Day was not the bloodiest battle of World War II, but it was one of the most important. The war was the most devastating event in world history. It claimed more than 50 million lives and affected the world like no other conflict before or since.[5] Without Allied success on D-Day and victory in the Battle of Normandy, the war could have followed a significantly different course.

On June 6, 1964, retired US president Dwight D. Eisenhower participated in an interview held at Omaha Beach, where 20 years earlier his soldiers

D-DAY ON THE HOME FRONT

In the United States, people learned about the Normandy invasion on their radios. Church bells tolled, stores and theaters closed, sporting events were canceled, and churches were packed. President Roosevelt declared June 6 a national day of prayer. He went on the radio to deliver a prayer himself, asking for divine protection for "our sons, the pride of our nation."[6] But real news about the progress of the invasion was slow to come. Casualty details, the information people wanted most, were not released to the public until long after the event.

successfully seized a beachhead at a high cost. He reflected on the importance of the invasion:

> [I]t's a wonderful thing to remember what those fellows twenty years ago were fighting for and sacrificing for, what they did to preserve our way of life. Not to conquer any territory, for any ambitions of their own. But to make sure that Hitler could not destroy freedom in the world. . . . To think of the lives that were given for that principle, paying a terrible price on this beach alone, on that day, 2,000 casualties. But they did it so that the world could be free.[7]

Normandy's solemn cemeteries, featuring rows and rows of headstones inscribed with the names of thousands of people who gave their lives there, are a striking reminder of the sacrifices made on D-Day.

Eisenhower, *right*, and reporter Walter Cronkite returned to Normandy for an interview.

TIMELINE

1940
In June, France surrenders to Germany.

1941
Germany declares war on the United States in December.

1942
Canadian troops carry out a disastrous raid on Dieppe, France, in August.

1943
Field Marshal Erwin Rommel takes charge of the Atlantic Wall in November.

1944
On June 6, at 6:30 a.m., US Army troops land at Utah and Omaha Beaches.

1944
On the morning of June 6, British troops land at Gold and Sword Beaches.

1944
On the morning of June 6, Canadian divisions land at Juno Beach.

1944
After landing on June 6, soldiers from the US Army Rangers capture Pointe du Hoc.

1944
Dwight Eisenhower gives the final go-ahead order on June 5.

1944
In the early morning of June 6, the first airborne troops begin parachute drops into the Normandy countryside.

1944
On June 6, British glider troops take Pegasus Bridge soon after landing.

1944
At 3:00 a.m. on June 6, gliders land reinforcements in Normandy.

1944
In the afternoon of June 6, troops begin securing and moving off of Omaha Beach.

1944
The Allies secure the five beachheads within a week of D-Day.

1944
Allied armies begin breaking out of Normandy in late July during Operation Cobra.

1945
The Allies formally accept the unconditional surrender of Nazi Germany on May 8.

ESSENTIAL FACTS

KEY PLAYERS

- Dwight David Eisenhower is Supreme Commander of Allied Expeditionary Forces, in charge of all aspects of D-Day and the Battle of Normandy.

- Erwin Rommel is the German field marshal in charge of building the Atlantic Wall.

- Adolf Hitler is the leader of Nazi Germany.

- Winston Churchill, prime minister of the United Kingdom, works closely with US president Franklin D. Roosevelt in establishing the grand strategy that leads to D-Day.

KEY STATISTICS

- Hitler's Atlantic Wall stretched for approximately 3,000 miles (4,800 km) around the coast of occupied Europe.

- Approximately 175,000 soldiers and 5,000 ships and landing craft participated in the D-Day invasion.

- More than 10,000 Allied aircraft filled the skies over Normandy on D-Day.

- Approximately 4,900 Allied soldiers were killed or wounded on D-Day.

KEY WEAPONS AND TECHNOLOGIES

- The Atlantic Wall was an elaborate system of defenses and barriers built by the Germans along hundreds of miles of the Atlantic coast of Europe. It included thousands of steel-reinforced bunkers that protected large guns and soldiers. At Normandy these fortifications withstood the heaviest bombs and shells the Allies had, and many are still standing today.

- The Allies used thousands of landing craft to bring troops, supplies, and equipment ashore on D-Day. Beach landings would not have been possible without the small, flat-bottomed craft known as Higgins Boats.

IMPACT ON HISTORY

D-Day and the Normandy invasion, among the largest military operations in history, led directly to the surrender of Germany eleven months later. Without D-Day, World War II might have lasted much longer, resulting in greater death and destruction.

QUOTE

"Every obstacle must be overcome, every inconvenience suffered, and every risk run to ensure that our blow is decisive. We cannot afford to fail."

—Dwight D. Eisenhower

GLOSSARY

ARMADA
A fleet of warships.

BARGE
A flat-bottomed boat designed to carry heavy loads.

BARRAGE
A large, coordinated artillery attack.

BLUFF
A steep hill or cliff.

CASEMATE
A fortified structure from which guns can be fired.

CASUALTY
A person who is injured, missing, or killed, during a military campaign.

COMMANDO
A highly skilled soldier trained to carry out raids separately from a main military force.

FANATICAL
Having obsessive interest and enthusiasm for a political cause.

FLAK
Antiaircraft fire.

HEDGEROW
A narrow ridge of thick brush that served as a fence between fields in Normandy and elsewhere.

PILLBOX
An enclosed concrete structure used as a defensive outpost.

TRACER BULLET
Ammunition that produces a visible trail when fired, used to help make aiming corrections.

ADDITIONAL RESOURCES

SELECTED BIBLIOGRAPHY

Beevor, Antony. *D-Day: The Battle for Normandy*. New York: Viking, 2009. Print.

Penrose, Jane, ed. *The D-Day Companion: Leading Historians Explore History's Greatest Amphibious Assault*. Oxford, UK: Osprey, 2004. Print.

Tillman, Barrett. *Brassey's D-Day Encyclopedia: The Normandy Invasion A-Z*. Washington, DC: Brassey's, 2004. Print.

FURTHER READINGS

Adams, Simon. *World War II*. New York: DK, 2014. Print.

Atkinson, Rick. *D-Day: The Invasion of Normandy*. New York: Holt, 2014. Print.

WEBSITES

To learn more about Essential Library of World War II, visit **booklinks.abdopublishing.com**. These links are routinely monitored and updated to provide the most current information available.

PLACES TO VISIT

D-Day Museum
Place du 6 Juin
14117 Arromanches, France
http://www.arromanches-museum.com/accueil/index.php?lang=uk
This museum is located overlooking Gold Beach, where the first artificial Mulberry harbor was built. Its remains can still be seen there today, just offshore.

National World War II Museum
945 Magazine Street
New Orleans, LA 70130
504-528-1944
http://nationalww2museum.org
This museum is located in New Orleans, not far from the place Higgins boats were built. Interactive exhibits allow visitors to experience the war firsthand. One lets you walk among Normandy's dense hedgerows and imagine the challenges soldiers faced on D-Day.

SOURCE NOTES

CHAPTER 1. THUNDER OVER NORMANDY

1. "The Horsa." *Royal Air Force*. Royal Air Force, 2015. Web. 3 Apr. 2015.

2. Stephen Ambrose. *D-Day, June 6, 1941: The Climactic Battle of World War II*. New York: Simon, 1994. Print. 20–21.

CHAPTER 2. DANGEROUS TIMES, DESPERATE MEASURES

1. Winston Churchill. "The Few." *Speeches*. The Churchill Centre, 2015. Web. 3 Apr. 2015.

2. Julian Thompson. "The Dieppe Raid." *BBC History*. BBC, 30 Mar. 2011. Web. 3 Apr. 2015.

3. Ibid.

4. Ibid.

5. "Messerschmitt Me 262A Schwalbe." *National Museum of the US Air Force*. US Air Force, 24 Oct. 2014. Web. 3 Apr. 2015.

6. Tony Rennell. "The 1688 Invasion of Britain That's Been Erased from History." *Daily Mail*. Daily Mail, 18 Apr. 2008. Web. 3 Apr. 2015.

7. Stephen Ambrose. *D-Day, June 6, 1941: The Climactic Battle of World War II*. New York: Simon, 1994. Print. 111.

CHAPTER 3. PLANNING THE INVASION

1. "D-Day: June 6, 1944." *National World War II Museum*. National World War II Museum, n.d. Web. 3 Apr. 2015.

2. "Strait of Dover." *Encyclopaedia Britannica*. Encyclopaedia Britannica, 2015. Web. 3 Apr. 2015.

3. Stephen Ambrose. *D-Day, June 6, 1941: The Climactic Battle of World War II*. New York: Simon, 1994. Print. 512-13.

4. Ibid. 133.

5. Ibid. 68.

6. Ibid. 162.

CHAPTER 4. A WAITING GAME

1. Stephen Ambrose. *D-Day, June 6, 1941: The Climactic Battle of World War II*. New York: Simon, 1994. Print. 170.

2. Ibid. 188.

CHAPTER 5. THE ASSAULT BEGINS

1. "General Dwight D. Eisenhower's Order of the Day." *Our Documents*. Our Documents, n.d. Web. 3 Apr. 2015.

2. Ronald J. Drez. *Twenty-Five Yards of War: The Extraordinary Courage of Ordinary Men in World War II*. New York: Hyperion, 2001. Print. 119.

3. Stephen Ambrose. *D-Day, June 6, 1941: The Climactic Battle of World War II*. New York: Simon, 1994. Print. 196.

4. John Keegan. *Six Armies in Normandy: From D-Day to the Liberation of Paris*. New York: Penguin, 1994. Print. 81–85.

5. Stephen Ambrose. *D-Day, June 6, 1941: The Climactic Battle of World War II*. New York: Simon, 1994. Print. 175, 216.

6. Ibid. 217–218.

7. *The D-Day Companion: Leading Historians Explore History's Greatest Amphibious Assault*. Jane Penrose, Ed. Oxford, UK: Osprey, 2004. Print. 203–204.

8. Stephen Ambrose. *D-Day, June 6, 1941: The Climactic Battle of World War II*. New York: Simon, 1994. Print. 217–218.

9. Ibid. 63.

CHAPTER 6. THE FLEET ARRIVES

1. Stephen Ambrose. *D-Day, June 6, 1941: The Climactic Battle of World War II*. New York: Simon, 1994. Print. 248.

2. Ibid. 253.

3. Ibid. 224.

SOURCE NOTES
CONTINUED

CHAPTER 7. THE AMERICAN BEACHES

1. "D-Day and the Battle of Normandy: Your Questions Answered." *D-Day Museum*. D-Day Museum, 2014. Web. 3 Apr. 2015.

2. Stephen Ambrose. *D-Day, June 6, 1941: The Climactic Battle of World War II*. New York: Simon, 1994. Print. 331.

3. Ibid. 335.

4. "Andrew Jackson Higgins." *Higgins Memorial*. Higgins Memorial, n.d. Web. 3 Apr. 2015.

5. Douglas Brinkley. "The Man Who Won the War for Us." *American Heritage* 51.3 (May/June 2000): 49. Print.

6. "Pointe-du-Hoc Ranger Monument." *American Battle Monuments Commission*. American Battle Monuments Commission, n.d. Web. 3 Apr. 2015.

7. "D-Day and the Battle of Normandy: Your Questions Answered." *D-Day Museum*. D-Day Museum, 2014. Web. 3 Apr. 2015.

CHAPTER 8. JUNO, SWORD, AND GOLD

1. Stephen Ambrose. *D-Day, June 6, 1941: The Climactic Battle of World War II*. New York: Simon, 1994. Print. 538.

2. Mark Zuehlke. *Juno Beach: Canada's D-Day Victory—June 6, 1944*. Vancouver, BC: Douglas, 2004. Print. 337.

3. "D-Day and the Battle of Normandy: Your Questions Answered." *D-Day Museum*. D-Day Museum, 2014. Web. 3 Apr. 2015.

4. Ibid.

5. Barrett Tillman. *Brassey's D-Day Encyclopedia: The Normandy Invasion A-Z*. Washington, DC: Brassey's, 2004. Print. 164.

CHAPTER 9. THE ALLIES PREVAIL

1. "Falaise." *Encyclopaedia Britannica*. Encyclopaedia Britannica, 2015. Web. 3 Apr. 2015.

2. "D-Day Anniversary: 'World-Changing' Day Remembered." *BBC News*. BBC, 6 June 2014. Web. 3 Apr. 2015.

3. "D-Day." *American Experience*. PBS, 2015. Web. 3 Apr. 2015.

4. "D-Day Anniversary: 'World-Changing' Day Remembered." *BBC News*. BBC, 6 June 2014. Web. 3 Apr. 2015.

5. *The D-Day Companion: Leading Historians Explore History's Greatest Amphibious Assault*. Jane Penrose, Ed. Oxford, UK: Osprey, 2004. Print. 203–204.

6. "Franklin Roosevelt's D-Day Prayer." *Our Documents*. Our Documents, n.d. Web. 3 Apr. 2015.

7. Stephen Ambrose. *D-Day, June 6, 1941: The Climactic Battle of World War II*. New York: Simon, 1994. Print. 583.

INDEX

ABOUT THE AUTHOR

Michael Capek is a retired teacher and the author of numerous books for young readers, including *Stonehenge*, part of Abdo's Digging Up the Past series. Stories his father told about his adventures in Europe during World War II helped instill in Michael a deep appreciation for history and war veterans. Michael lives in northern Kentucky with his wife and two children.